SELENA

GOMEZ

POP STAR AND ACTRESS

For Maren,
who let me watch TV with her
and call it research

Lerner Publications Company
A division of Lerner Publishing Group, Inc.
241 First Avenue North
Minneapolis, MN 55401 U.S.A.

Website address: www.lernerbooks.com

Library of Congress Cataloging-in-Publication Data

Nelson, Robin, 1971–
    Selena Gomez : pop star and actress / by Robin Nelson.
        p.   cm. — (Pop culture bios: super singers)
    Includes bibliographical references and index.
    ISBN 978–0–7613–4142–0 (lib. bdg. : alk. paper)
    1. Gomez, Selena, 1992– —Juvenile literature.
  2. Actors—United States—Biography—Juvenile literature.
  3. Singers—United States—Biography—Juvenile literature.
  I. Title.
  PN2287.G585N47 2013
  791.4302'8092—dc23 [B]   2011044683

Manufactured in the United States of America
1 – PC – 7/15/12

INTRODUCTION PAGE 4

CHAPTER ONE
GROWING UP IN TEXAS
PAGE 8

CHAPTER TWO
THE MAGIC OF DISNEY
PAGE 14

CHAPTER THREE
MOVIES, MUSIC, AND MORE
PAGE 18

CHAPTER FOUR
FAME AND THE FUTURE
PAGE 24

SELENA PICS!   28
SOURCE NOTES   30
MORE SELENA INFO   30
INDEX   31

INTRODUCTION

On May 14, 2011, Selena Gomez sent out this tweet to her fans:

"Jake, myself and David. Our last walk to set....
I love you @jaketaustin and @David_henrie.
We wrap today."

The tweet was about the wrap of *Wizards of Waverly Place*. Selena starred in this superpopular Disney Channel show alongside Jake T. Austin and David Henrie. The talented trio grew up together on the set. They worked hard—but they also cracked each other up! Selena would so miss seeing her costars every day.

Selena glammed up for a movie premiere in February 2011.

After the wrap, Selena dished with *Access Hollywood* about filming that last show. **"It was so emotional!"** she gushed. "I kept crying and I'm still kind of, like, shaky right now."

WRAP =
the end of a filming schedule

Wizards of Waverly Place wasn't Selena's first acting job. But it was the show that launched her into superstardom.

Selena knows she owes her success on the show to her fans. At the 2010 Teen Choice Awards, her fans voted her Choice TV Actress in the comedy category. When she accepted her award, she said, "Thank you so much. This award is [for] you guys who watch our show."

Selena pauses for a pic on the red carpet at a charity concert in 2011.

In 2007, when she first started filming *Wizards*, Selena had no idea what a big star she would become. In her wildest dreams, she never would've thought she'd act in movies, sing, and even design clothes. She just knew she loved performing for an audience. **"I get to be challenged, and I get to be artistically a different person,"** Selena says of performing. It was all she ever wanted to do.

Selena dedicated her 2010 Teen Choice Award to her cast and to everyone who watches her show.

Selena and her mom, Mandy

CHAPTER ONE
GROWING UP IN TEXAS

Selena and her best friend, Demi Lovato

Selena Marie Gomez was born on July 22, 1992. Her mom, Amanda (Mandy) Cornett, and her dad, Ricardo Gomez, were practically kids themselves when she was born. Mandy was sixteen and Ricardo was seventeen when Mandy had Selena. The young couple eventually got married.

Selena grew up in Grand Prairie, Texas. Since her parents were still in high school, Selena's grandma and grandpa helped raise her. Selena called them Nana and Papa. She was—and still is—super close to her grandparents.

WHAT'S IN A NAME?

Selena's dad was a huge fan of Latina singer Selena Quintanilla-Pérez (LEFT). The singer was a superstar in Mexico and in the United States. Selena's parents named their daughter after the singer. Sadly, Selena Quintanilla-Pérez was murdered by the disturbed president of her fan club in 1995. She was only twenty-three when she died.

Selena Gomez was named after singer Selena Quintanilla-Pérez. In this pic, the fabulous Latina star shows off her Grammy Award.

When Selena was five, her parents divorced. **"It was really hard. I remember just being really angry,"** Selena said in an E! special. She wanted her family to stay together. After the divorce, Selena and her mom moved to an apartment. They didn't have much money. And Selena missed seeing her dad every day.

Selena's mom liked to act in plays. Selena went with her mom when she rehearsed for the plays. She watched as Mandy put on stage makeup. Selena was totally taken with the hustle and bustle she saw as actors prepared to perform. She told her mom that she wanted to act too.

A Big Break and a BFF

On her seventh birthday, Selena tried out for a role on the kids' TV show *Barney & Friends*. The show was filmed

LATINA STAR

Selena's mom is Italian. Her dad's family is from Mexico. Selena is proud of her heritage. Her family isn't super traditional, but they do celebrate *quinceañeras*. They also have barbecues in the park on Sundays after church—another Latin American custom. Selena loves taking part in traditions like these.

QUINCEAÑERA =
a special fifteenth-birthday
bash thrown for a Latina girl

in Dallas, Texas. When Selena got to the tryout, fourteen hundred other kids were also waiting to audition! As she was waiting for her turn, she noticed a girl standing in front of her. They started talking. The girl asked Selena if she wanted to color while they waited. So they sat down in line and colored. The girl's name was Demi Lovato. The girls had no clue that they'd become best friends and stars! Both Selena and Demi landed parts on *Barney*.

AUDITION =
to try out for a part

This cast photo shows Selena (ON YELLOW BALL) and Demi (ON BLUE BALL) on the set of *Barney* in 2004.

Selena played the role of Gianna. She loved being on the show. She and Demi had tons of fun talking and laughing together on the set. But at school, kids teased her for being on a show for babies. She cried a lot and didn't want to go to school.

Mandy made Selena go to school anyway.

But whenever Selena came home upset, her mom would comfort her and make her feel better. And in spite of all the teasing, Selena still adored her job. She couldn't get enough of acting!

Selena's mom, Mandy, totally supports her daughter.

Moving On

After playing Gianna for two years, Selena was too old to be on *Barney*. Once she left the show, she started working with an acting coach in Dallas. Whenever she went to a tryout, Selena was really nervous. Sometimes she would shake and sweat. But her coach helped her learn to relax. She told her to chill out and have fun in each tryout. Her advice really helped Selena.

3RD MISSION. 3RD DIMENSION.

SPY KIDS 3-D
GAME OVER

COMING AT YOU JULY 25TH   DIMENSION

AWESOMENESS ON-SCREEN

Selena had several awesome acting opportunities right after her time on *Barney* ended. These included roles in *Spy Kids 3-D: Game Over* and the TV film *Walker, Texas Ranger: Trial by Fire*.

Selena appeared in the film *Spy Kids 3-D: Game Over* in 2003.

CHAPTER TWO

THE MAGIC OF DISNEY

Selena on the set of
Wizards of Waverly Place

In March 2004, Selena and her mom went to Austin, Texas. They'd learned that the Disney Channel was holding nationwide tryouts there. Kids who did well might get a chance to be on a Disney show. Selena, of course, was all over that opportunity!

Her tryout must have gone well. Disney called her just a week later. They wanted to fly her to Los Angeles, California, for a screen test.

Selena went over and over and *over* her lines on the plane. But when she left the screen test, she didn't think she'd given a good performance. She went to her mom and bawled.

SCREEN TEST =
a tryout where an actor reads lines while being filmed

But Selena was wrong. The people at Disney loved her! They cast her in a new show. Unfortunately, the show never made it on TV.

Still, Disney knew Selena was special. They found other parts for her. In 2006, she played a small part on the Disney Channel series *The Suite Life of Zack & Cody*. She was scared to play the part. It was her first time filming in front of a live audience. And she had to kiss Dylan Sprouse, who played Zack, while the whole audience watched!

To top it all off, it was the first time she'd ever kissed a boy. "I leaned in to kiss him," Selena remembered, "and I had my eyes closed a little too early and I ended up missing, like, half of his lip. **So it ended up being the most awkward kiss in the world!**"

Becoming a Wizard

Selena tried out for a new Disney television series later in 2004. It was called *Wizards of Waverly Place.* Selena's character, Alex Russo, was one of three family members who are wizards in training.

Wizards was filmed in L.A. So Selena and her mom moved there. But before moving, Selena's mom married her boyfriend, Brian Teefey.

Moving to L.A. was really hard for Selena. She'd grown up in Texas surrounded by family and friends. Now she wouldn't see them as much. She had to say good-bye to her dad, her grandparents, and her friends.

Selena also had to adjust to a crazy busy work schedule. She got up at 5 A.M. and was on the *Wizards* set until 5 P.M. every day. She didn't have time to go to a regular school anymore, so she attended classes on the set. But the hard work paid off. *Wizards* premiered on October, 12, 2007, to 5.9 million viewers! Fans adored the show. Selena was thrilled that audiences were showing *Wizards* so much love.

CHAPTER THREE

MOVIES, MUSIC, AND MORE

Selena and *Another Cinderella Story* costar Drew Seeley

Selena continued to film *Wizards*. But she looked for other projects too. In 2008, she filmed a TV movie called *Another Cinderella Story*. She had to dance in the film. She took dancing lessons to get ready. The movie producers also wanted her to sing. They thought Selena had star singing potential. She'd already recorded some songs for Disney, including the theme song for *Wizards*. The producers liked what they'd heard and wanted to hear more. Selena did an amazing job singing songs for the new film.

Selena played an awesome dancer and got to sing in 2008's *Another Cinderella Story*.

ANOTHER FAB FLICK

Another Cinderella Story wasn't the only movie Selena was involved in back in 2008. She also provided the voices of the Mayor of Who-ville's daughters in the animated film *Horton Hears a Who!* Giving these characters their voices was no easy feat—because the Mayor of Who-ville has ninety-six daughters! They each have their own personality. Selena had to come up with many different voices for the characters.

19

With that in mind, Selena became involved in the UR Votes Count campaign in 2008. She visited 150 malls all over the country to encourage kids to learn about the election. "Being a teen myself, I think we [need to be] educated on the issues that affect us all, so when we're eligible, we're fully prepared to take on one of our greatest privileges and responsibilities—voting," explained Selena.

Selena also became the youngest ambassador (spokesperson) for UNICEF. UNICEF provides food, water,

Selena likes to give back. In 2008, she helped kick off the annual Trick-or-Treat for UNICEF campaign. UNICEF helps kids around the world.

and education to kids around the world. Selena traveled to Ghana in West Africa on a mission with UNICEF.

Awards

In the fall of 2009, Selena began filming the third season of *Wizards*. The show later won an Emmy for Outstanding Children's Program.

A week after *Wizards* won the Emmy, Selena Gomez & the Scene released their first album called *Kiss & Tell*. Selena was thrilled when the album sold sixty-six thousand copies in the first week! Selena Gomez & the Scene went on tour to perform their music. Selena raved about the tour, saying **"Touring is the best experience. My fans mean the world to me."**

The cast and producers celebrate *Wizards'* 2009 Emmy win for Outstanding Children's Program.

CHAPTER FOUR

FAME AND THE FUTURE

Selena and Justin Bieber

Selena had become superfamous. But that meant she didn't have much privacy. Paparazzi trailed her everywhere she went. Whenever she was seen with a boy, rumors flew that they were dating. This was hard for Selena. She would put in her headphones and listen to music so she couldn't hear the paparazzi shouting things like, "Who's your boyfriend?" and "Are you dating anyone?"

PAPARAZZI = *celebrity photographers*

BOYS, BOYS, BOYS

Rumors have linked Selena to several famous boys, including Nick Jonas and Taylor Lautner. But Selena has always been very private about her personal life. Then, in 2010, she was seen with music superstar Justin Bieber. They had been friends for a while. But now they were spotted eating ice cream together, dancing, and even smooching in Hawaii. They also posted pictures of each other online. But they never admitted they were dating. Finally, the two announced in February 2011 that they were a couple. Selena wore Justin's favorite color—purple—to the premiere of his movie *Never Say Never*. And they appeared at an awards party holding hands. Fans gave the cute pair the nickname Jelena.

Selena's family and friends keep her from getting too caught up in the craziness of Hollywood. Selena especially loves and respects her mom. Her mom and stepdad treat her like a regular person, not like a diva. When she was growing up, they didn't allow her to be wild and crazy. They made her do laundry and help with dishes.

Look on the Awesome Side!

Focusing on the awesome parts about being a star also helps Selena deal with her crazy life. She especially loved getting the chance to attend the premiere for *Ramona and Beezus* in 2010. It was her first big film premiere. And she was thrilled when Kmart invited her to launch a new clothing line for their stores. The fun and flirty line is called Dream Out Loud by Selena Gomez. Another highlight of the year was the release of Selena Gomez & the Scene's second album, *A Year Without Rain*.

SELENA'S FACEBOOK STATUS

OCTOBER 20, 2011

"Flipping through some fashion mags... getting some inspiration for my next *Dream Out Loud* Collection. High-waisted shorts or skirts—which do you like better?"

Selena makes notes in sketchbooks showing her Dream Out Loud clothing collection.

All Grown Up

In 2011, Selena looked toward life after *Wizards.* She hopes her fans will continue to support and follow her. With tons of new projects to help keep her image fresh, chances are that Selena's not going anywhere. In June 2011, her band released yet another hit album, *When the Sun Goes Down.* They also began their first headlining tour. They played to audiences in countries all over the world.

In July 2011, fans got to see Selena star in the movie *Monte Carlo.* Selena played two parts— the main character, Grace, and an heiress. She also made a cameo appearance in *The Muppets,* which came to theaters in November. Selena even started her own production company. It's called July Moon Productions. With her company, she hopes to make movies she really cares about. Fans haven't heard the last from Selena Gomez!

HEADLINING = being the main act in a show

CAMEO = a brief appearance in a show

SELENA GOMEZ & The SCENE

WHEN THE SUN GOES DOWN

SELENA PICS!

Leighton Meester, Selena, and Katie Cassidy in a scene from *Monte Carlo*

Selena and the rest of the cast of
Wizards at the 2010 Teen Choice Awards

SOURCE NOTES

5   Selena Gomez, Twitter post, May 14, 2011, http://twitter.com/#!/selenagomez/
     status/69438168608411648 (November 28, 2011).

6   Selena Gomez, "Selena Gomez on the End of 'Wizards of Waverly Place' I Was 'So
     Emotional,' *Access Hollywood*, YouTube, posted by Asho860, May 17, 2011, http://www
     .youtube.com/watch?v=JKIXir-quro&NR=1 (October 22, 2011).

6   Selena Gomez, "Selena Gomez Wins Choice Teen TV Actress, Comedy—Teen Choice
     Awards 2010," YouTube, posted by MissSelGomezFANS, August 10, 2010, http://www
     .youtube.com/watch?NR=1&v=qu7gJgKqLUs (October 22, 2011).

7   Selena Gomez, "K104 Interviews Selena Gomez at Bethal Woods 8.5.11," YouTube,
     posted by pamalwebmaster, August 11, 2011, http://www.youtube.com
     /watch?v=MYE8hkoWOEQ (November 12, 2011).

10   "E! Entertainment Special: Selena Gomez," E! Entertainment Television, June 29, 2011.

16   Selena Gomez, "Selena Gomez Talks about Her Awkward First Kiss with Dylan Sprouse,"
     popdirt.com, January 20, 2009, http://popdirt.com/selena-gomez-talks-about-her
     -awkward-first-kiss-with-dylan-sprouse/71310/ (November 12, 2011).

21–22 Audrey Fine, "Selena Gomez Talks to Teen," *Seventeen*, n.d., http://www.seventeen.com
     /entertainment/features/selena-gomez-interview-2 (November 28, 2011).

22   Liz Perle, "Under 18? Vote with Selena Gomez!" electionista blog, *Seventeen*, August 19,
     2008, http://www.seventeen.com/college-career-old/teen-voting-elections-blog/selena
     -gomez-ur-votes-count (November 28, 2011).

23   "E! Entertainment Special: Selena Gomez."

MORE SELENA INFO

Azzarelli, Ally. *Selena Gomez: Latina TV and Music Star*. Berkeley Heights, NJ: Enslow, 2012. Learn
more about Selena Gomez, her movies, her love life, and her band.

The Disney Channel
http://disney.go.com/disneychannel
Watch videos, play games, and read up on *Wizards of Waverly Place* and other Disney shows.

Donovan, Sandy. *The Hispanic American Experience*. Minneapolis: Twenty-First Century Books, 2011.
Find out more about the Latino culture that has been an important part of Selena's life.

Edwards, Posy. *Selena Gomez*. London: Orion Publishing Group, 2011.
This picture-filled scrapbook pays tribute to Selena, giving her admirers an inside peek at her life
in front of and behind the cameras.

Higgins, Nadia. *Justin Bieber: Pop and R & B Idol*. Minneapolis: Lerner Publications Company, 2013.
Get the scoop on Justin Bieber, pop music superstar and Selena's beloved BF.

Selena Gomez
http://selenagomez.com
Check out Selena's official website for updates, information on her fan club, and messages from
Selena herself.

INDEX

Another Cinderella Story, 19
Austin, Jake T., 5

Barney & Friends, 10–13
Bieber, Justin, 25

Cornett, Amanda (Mandy), 9–10, 12, 15–16, 26

Disney Channel, 5, 15–16, 19–20
Dream Out Loud by Selena Gomez, 26

Gomez, Ricardo, 9–10, 17

Henrie, David, 5

July Moon Productions, 27

Lovato, Demi, 11–12, 20

Monte Carlo, 27

Muppets, The, 27

Princess Protection Program, 20

Quintanilla-Pérez, Selena, 9

Ramona and Beezus, 20, 26

Selena Gomez & the Scene, 21, 23, 26–27
Sprouse, Dylan, 15–16
Suite Life of Zack & Cody, The, 15

Teen Choice Awards, 6, 20

UNICEF, 23
UR Votes Count campaign, 22

Wizards of Waverly Place, 5–7, 16–17, 19, 23, 27
Wizards of Waverly Place: The Movie, 20

PHOTO ACKNOWLEDGMENTS

The images in this book are used with the permission of: © Larry Busacca/Getty Images, pp. 2, 24 (top right); © Michael Tran/FilmMagic/Getty Images, pp. 3 (top), 8 (top), 12; © Mark Sullivan/WireImage/Getty Images, pp. 3 (bottom), 24 (bottom); © Arthur Mola/CORBIS, p. 4 (top left); © Brian To/FilmMagic/Getty Images, p. 4 (top right); AP Photo/Chris Pizzello, p. 4 (bottom); © Jason Merritt/Getty Images, p. 5; © Angela Weiss/Getty Images, p. 6; © Kevin Winter/Getty Images, pp. 7, 18 (bottom right); © K Mazur/WireImage/Getty Images, p. 8 (bottom); © Mitchell Gerber/CORBIS, p. 9; © Hit Entertainment/Courtesy Everett Collection, p. 11; © Dimension Films/Courtesy Everett Collection, p. 13; © Rena Durham/Retna Ltd, p. 14 (left); © Disney Channel/Courtesy Everett Collection, p. 14 (right); © Alexandra Wyman/WireImage/Getty Images, p. 16; © John Shearer/WireImage/Getty Images, p. 18 (top); Alex J. Berliner/BEImages/Rex USA, p. 18 (bottom left); © Warner Premiere/Courtesy Everett Collection, p. 19 (top); TM and © Copyright Twentieth Century Fox. All rights reserved/Courtesy Everett Collection, p. 19 (bottom); © Walt Disney/Everett Collection/Rex USA, p. 20; © Mario Castillo/Jam Media/LatinContent/Getty Images, p. 21; © Brian Ach/WireImage/Getty Images, p. 22; © Jason LaVeris/FilmMagic/Getty Images, p. 23; © Neil Mockford/FilmMagic/Getty Images, p. 24 (top left); A. Macpherson/T. Gillis/Splash News/Newscom, p. 25; © Albert Michael/Startraksphoto.com, p. 26; © Gareth Cattermole/Getty Images, p. 27; AP Photo/Hollywood Records, p. 28 (top left); Larry Horricks/© Fox 2000 Pictures/TM and Copyright 20th Century Fox Film Corp. All Rights Reserved/Courtesy Everett Collection, p. 28 (bottom left); © Stephen Lovekin/Getty Images, p. 28 (right); © JB Lacroix/WireImage/Getty Images, p. 29 (top left); © Jeff Kravitz/FilmMagic/Getty Images, p. 29 (top center); © Jordan Strauss/WireImage/Getty Images, p. 29 (right); © Kevin Mazur/WireImage/Getty Images, p. 29 (bottom).

Front cover: © Ethan Miller/Getty Images (left); © Jason LaVeris/FilmMagic/Getty Images (right).
Back cover: © Angela Weiss/Getty Images.

Main body text set in Shannon Std Book 12/18.
Typeface provided by Monotype Typography.

Materials provided by

Partnerships for Change,

a program of the California

State Library and supported

by the Library Services and

Construction Act.

PARTNERSHIPS FOR CHANGE

Un libro de Dorling Kindersley

Concebido, editado y diseñado por DK Direct Limited

Nota para los padres

¿Qué tienen dentro las naves espaciales? se ha concebido para ayudar a los niños a entender las maravillas de los viajes espaciales. Les muestra cómo entra un cohete en el espacio, a qué se parece el viajar en un módulo lunar y cómo se las arreglan los astronautas para pasar meses en una estación espacial. Es un libro para que usted y su hijo lo lean, comenten y disfruten juntos.

Editora Hilary Hockman
Diseñadoras Helen Spencer y Juliette Norsworthy
Diseñador tipográfico Nigel Coath

Ilustrador Richard Ward
Fotógrafos Geoff Dann y James Stevenson
Escrito por Alexandra Parsons
Asesor Nicholas Booth
Director de diseño Ed Day
Director editorial Jonathan Reed

Publicado por primera vez en Gran Bretaña en 1992
por Dorling Kindersley Limited,
9 Henrietta Street, London WC2E 8PS

ISBN 84-481-0208-8 (Obra completa)
ISBN 84-486-0012-6 (Volumen 15)

Printed in Italy

¿QUE TIENEN DENTRO?
LAS NAVES ESPACIALES

INTERAMERICANA · McGRAW-HILL
HEALTHCARE GROUP
NUEVA YORK · ST. LOUIS · SAN FRANCISCO · AUCKLAND
BOGOTÁ · CARACAS · LISBOA · LONDRES · MADRID · MÉXICO
MILÁN · MONTREAL · NUEVA DELHI · PARÍS · SAN JUAN
SINGAPUR · SYDNEY · TOKYO · TORONTO

EL COHETE

Este cohete Saturno 5 estadounidense llevó a los primeros astronautas a la Luna. Para entrar en el espacio tuvo que atravesar e aire a muchísima velocidad, y librarse de la gravedad terrestre (la fuerza que tira de las cosas hacia la Tierra). Luego siguió impulsándose por el vacío.

El Saturno 5 eran tres cohetes en uno. La primera fase llevó a todo el cohete por el aire hasta el límite con el espacio. Luego se desprendió.

La tercera fase era la más pequeña pero la más importante. ¡Llevaba a los astronautas!

La segunda fase tomó el relevo de la primera. Cuando la segunda fase se quedó sin combustible, se desprendió.

Esta es la cámara de combustión, donde de verdad se calientan las cosas. El queroseno y el oxígeno llegan de los depósitos de combustible, se juntan aquí y... ¡bang! Salen unas llamas enormes, que elevan más y más el cohete.

Los tres astronautas van aquí, en el módulo base. Es sorprendentemente pequeño, en comparación con el cohete completo.

Como en el espacio no hay aire, tampoco hay oxígeno, así que cada fase tiene que llevar su propio suministro. Esto es el depósito de oxígeno.

Esto es el depósito de queroseno.

La gravedad sujeta las cosas a la Tierra. Sin ella, al dar un salto no volverías a la Tierra.

EL MODULO BASE

El módulo base y el módulo lunar sólo eran partes del cohete Saturno 5 que fue hasta la Luna. Los astronautas fueron y volvieron a la Luna dentro del módulo base.

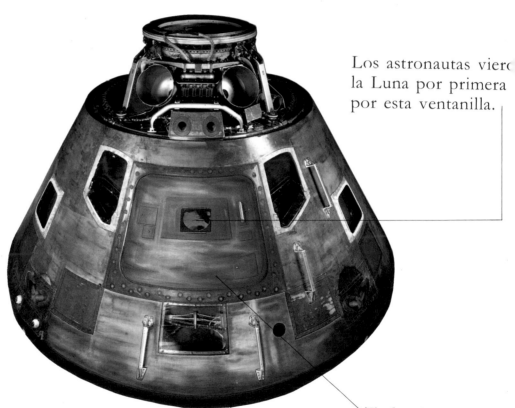

Los astronautas viero[n] la Luna por primera por esta ventanilla.

Todos los astronaut[as] volvieron a casa a salvo. Salieron por esta escotilla.

Una gruesa cubierta protegió al módulo base al volver al espacio y al entrar en la capa de aire que rodea a la Tierra. El módulo se calentó muchísimo al rozar contra el aire mientras caía.

¡Chop! Estos paracaídas disminuyeron la velocidad de caída del módulo en el mar. ¡Al amerizar salpicó mucho!

El módulo lunar llevó a los astronautas hasta la superficie lunar. Iba acoplado aquí. La tripulación gateaba por este espacio para entrar desde el módulo base.

Estos son sólo dos de los motores que se usaron para guiar la nave.

Los astronautas no iban sentados en sus asientos. Iban tumbados para que no sintieran eso tan gracioso que a veces te pasa cuando montas en la montaña rusa.

El panel de instrumentos, con montones de complicados botones y pantallas, estaba fijado al techo.

EL MODULO LUNAR

Neil Armstrong y Buzz Aldrin fueron los primeros en pisar la Luna.
Alunizaron con este módulo lunar el 20 de Julio de 1969.

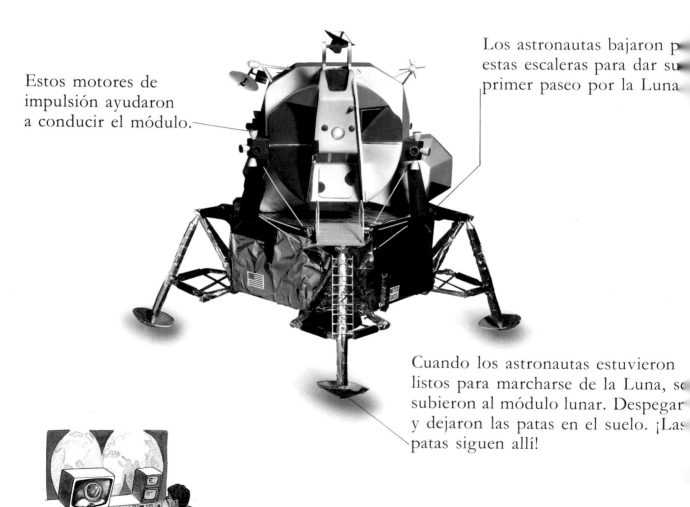

Los astronautas bajaron p
estas escaleras para dar su
primer paseo por la Luna

Estos motores de
impulsión ayudaron
a conducir el módulo.

Cuando los astronautas estuvieron
listos para marcharse de la Luna, se
subieron al módulo lunar. Despegar
y dejaron las patas en el suelo. ¡Las
patas siguen allí!

Las antenas de radio y televisión mantenían en contacto
a los astronautas con el módulo base, y con la estación
terrestre a miles de kilómetros.

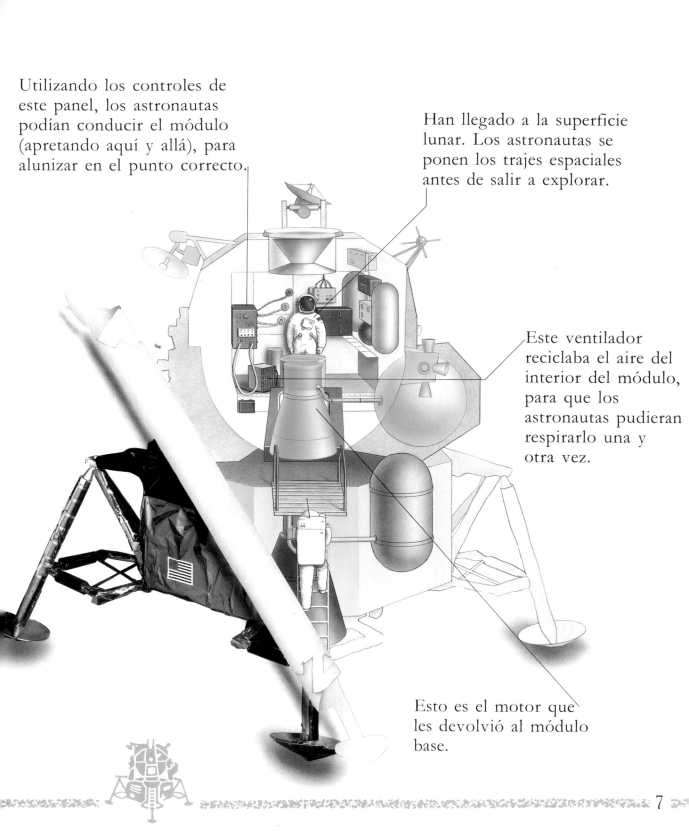

Utilizando los controles de este panel, los astronautas podían conducir el módulo (apretando aquí y allá), para alunizar en el punto correcto.

Han llegado a la superficie lunar. Los astronautas se ponen los trajes espaciales antes de salir a explorar.

Este ventilador reciclaba el aire del interior del módulo, para que los astronautas pudieran respirarlo una y otra vez.

Esto es el motor que les devolvió al módulo base.

EL TRAJE ESPACIAL

Nadie puede sobrevivir en el espacio sin un traje espacial. Tiene su propio depósito de aire, para que los astronautas puedan respirar. También les protege de los dañinos rayos del Sol, y de los trozos de roca que vuelan por el espacio.

Esta mochila se llama SPS: sistema portátil de supervivencia. Dentro hay oxígeno, agua, un transmisor de radio y un montón de importantes cables y tubos.

Esto es el panel de control del SPS.

El traje espacial tiene oxígeno y agua suficientes como para mantener con vida al astronauta durante 6 horas.

¡Las auténticas botas lunares! Van reforzadas con un metal que pesa mucho, para que sea posible caminar por la Luna.

Así que, ¿qué encontraron los astronautas cuando alunizaron? Gracias a las muestras de rocas que recogieron, sabemos que ahí arriba hay valiosos minerales, y puede que algún día haya minas en la Luna.

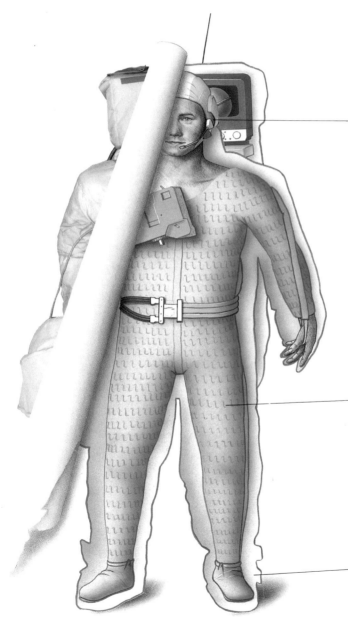

Dentro del casco hay un pequeño micrófono y unos auriculares, para que el astronauta esté en contacto con la base.

¿Cuánto tardas en vestirte por las mañanas? Neil Armstrong necesitó media hora para ponerse este traje, y además necesitó que le ayudaran.

Pasear por la Luna con un traje espacial da mucho calor. Por dentro lleva un sistema que transporta agua fría a todas partes, mediante pequeños tubos de plástico.

La cubierta externa está acolchada, para proteger frente a las rocas voladoras.

EL TRANSBORDADOR ESPACIAL

El transbordador es la forma moderna de dar la vuelta a la Tierra. Despega como un cohete y aterriza como un planeador. Hasta el espacio le impulsan dos cohetes y un ENORME depósito de combustible.

3..2..1. Cero.
¡Hemos despegado!

Los satélites se guardan plegados en contenedores especiales en la bodega, hasta que llegue el momento de lanzarlos.—

Las ventanillas de todo el transbordador tienen una cubierta especial, como unas gafas de sol, para protegerse de los dañinos rayos del Sol.—

Al volver a la Tierra, que está rodeada por una espesa capa de aire, el transbordador llega a ponerse incandescente. El transbordador tiene una cubierta especial para impedir que se derrita.—

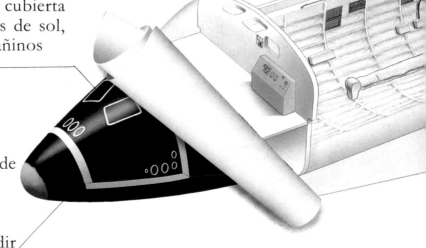

Las puertas de la bodega se abren hacia arriba. El transbordador puede seguir viajando por el espacio con ellas abiertas.

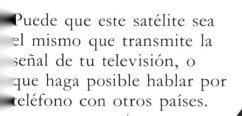

Puede que este satélite sea el mismo que transmite la señal de tu televisión, o que haga posible hablar por teléfono con otros países.

Estos motores dirigen al transbordador mientras flota en el espacio.

Este brazo saca los satélites con suavidad. Una vez que está flotando, las antenas, las parabólicas y los paneles solares se despliegan.

El transbordador tiene alas como un avión, porque aterriza aprovechando las corrientes de aire, igual que un planeador.

LA CABINA DEL TRANSBORDADOR

En un transbordador espacial pueden vivir y trabajar hasta ocho astronautas, mientras viajan por el espacio. Pueden quedarse allí durante aproximadamente una semana, haciendo experimentos, lanzando satélites y tomando fotos de las estrellas y los planetas. Su cabina está en el morro.

Imagina que intentas beber un vaso de zumo que no pesa. Si se sacan del contenedor, los líquidos flotan en forma de bola por todas partes; por eso los astronautas beben del envase, con una pajita.

No se puede comer comida normal: ¡no se queda quieta en el plato! Los astronautas comen en unos envases especiales. La comida es pegajosa, para que se pegue a la cuchara.

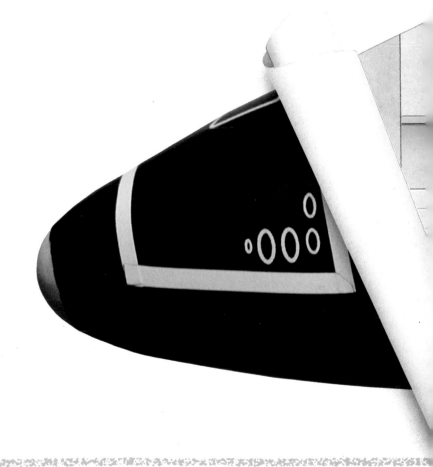

Dentro del transbordador, los astronautas llevan ropa normal. No tienen que llevar casco, porque la cabina está llena de aire normal.

Los astronautas que trabajan en el panel de control de la cabina de mandos no flotan porque están sujetos al suelo.

En el espacio no tiene sentido tumbarse, porque no hay arriba ni abajo. A la hora de acostarse, te metes en un saco y te cuelgas de un gancho de la pared, para no flotar mientras duermes.

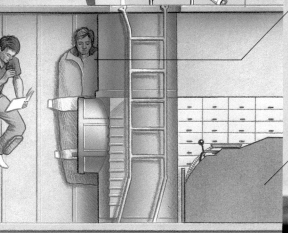

El retrete tiene unas agarraderas especiales, y utiliza corrientes de aire en lugar de agua para limpiarlo.

EL LABORATORIO ESPACIAL

El transbordador puede llevar en su bodega un laboratorio y un taller especiales. Se llama laboratorio espacial. En algunos vuelos, el laboratorio espacial lleva jaulas con monos y ratas, para que los científicos puedan estudiar la conducta de los animales en el espacio. O puede equiparse como un laboratorio médico para investigar sobre la fabricación de nuevas medicinas.

¿Vas a trabajar? Este túnel conecta la cabina del transbordador con el laboratorio espacial.

En la ingravidez del espacio, los científicos pueden hacer interesantes experimentos. Pueden fabricar metales especialmente fuertes que no se pueden fabricar en la Tierra.

En un laboratorio se llevaron arañas al espacio. Al principio no sabían cómo tejer la tela, pero aprendieron enseguida.

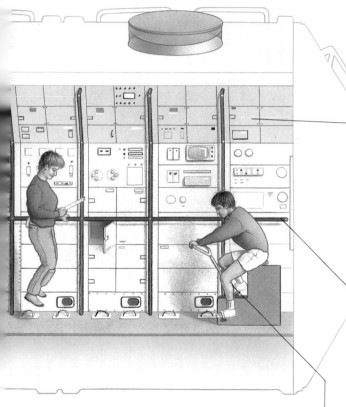

En el laboratorio espacial todo ha de estar cuidadosamente guardado, o se quedará flotando. ¡Hay cajones por todas partes!

Los bancos de trabajo llevan barandillas a los lados, por si los científicos se ponen a flotar mientras trabajan.

¡Hora de hacer ejercicio! Si flotas mucho tiempo en la ingravidez, los huesos y músculos se debilitan, porque no trabajan. Este aparato ayuda a los astronautas a mantenerse en forma.

LA ESTACION ESPACIAL

Esto es la estación espacial rusa Mir. Está formada por seis laboratorios unidos. Permanece todo el tiempo en el espacio, dando vueltas alrededor de la Tierra. Los astronautas van y vienen en naves especiales.

Los paneles solares recogen la energía del Sol y la emplean para fabricar la electricidad con la que funciona la estación.

La estación espacial es muy grande. Los astronautas permanecen meses en su interior.

La estación Mir tiene hasta un porche de entrada. Las naves visitantes aparcan aquí, para que los astronautas puedan ir y venir sin que se escape nada del valioso aire del interior.

Las antenas de radio y lo satélites mantienen en contacto a los astronauta con la base.

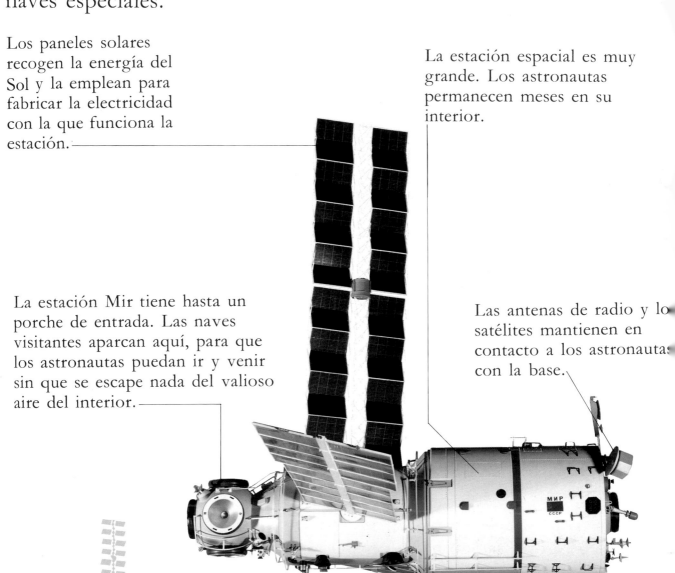